Original title:
When I Was Strong

Copyright © 2024 Swan Charm
All rights reserved.

Author: Linda Leevike
ISBN HARDBACK: 978-9916-89-948-9
ISBN PAPERBACK: 978-9916-89-949-6
ISBN EBOOK: 978-9916-89-950-2

Beneath the Angel's Wings

In silence deep, the angels sing,
A gentle peace their praises bring.
Wrapped in love, our spirits soar,
Beneath their wings, forevermore.

In trials faced, their light will guide,
With faith in hearts, we shall abide.
The burdens lift, the shadows flee,
For in their care, we are set free.

The Light Beyond Shadows

When darkness falls and hope seems lost,
The light appears, despite the cost.
With every step through fears we tread,
A path of grace, where angels led.

Beyond the veil, where spirits dance,
In sacred realms, we find our chance.
To rise above the worldly pain,
And feel the joy of love's sustain.

Transcending the Tempest

When storms arise and oceans churn,
Our hearts in faith to You shall turn.
For through the waves, the stillness speaks,
In every heart, Your presence seeks.

With whispered peace, You calm the night,
In darkest hours, You are our light.
Through trials fierce, we hold on tight,
Transcending strife, we find our flight.

Roots of Divine Strength

In sacred soil, our roots go deep,
Nurtured by faith, in dreams we reap.
The strength of love, it binds us true,
In every heart, a light anew.

With every storm, we stand as one,
United souls, 'neath moon and sun.
Together we shall rise and sing,
With roots of strength, our spirits bring.

Guided by the Divine

In the stillness, I seek Your light,
Heaven's whisper, soft and bright.
Each path I walk, I feel Your grace,
Holding my heart in this sacred space.

Moments of doubt, they come and go,
But Your love, like rivers, will flow.
Through shadows deep, I find my way,
Your guiding hand, my night and day.

Steadfast Through Storms

When thunder roars and the skies turn gray,
I stand my ground, come what may.
With faith as my anchor, I will not sway,
For in Your promise, I trust and pray.

Waves may crash, and fears arise,
Yet in my soul, Your peace complies.
Through trials fierce, my spirit grows,
In every tempest, Your wisdom shows.

A Fortress of Faith

Within my heart, a fortress strong,
Built by love, where I belong.
No fear can breach these sacred walls,
Your mighty presence ensures my calls.

With each prayer, the towers rise,
Guarding me as the world defies.
In unity, we stand as one,
Together shining, like the sun.

Devotion's Resolve

In moments dark, my spirit stays,
Rooted deep in holy ways.
With fervent heart, I bow and kneel,
Your grace surrounds, a sacred seal.

Each trial faced, I shall endure,
For in Your love, I am secure.
With faith as my compass, I will strive,
In devotion's path, my soul will thrive.

Divine Fortitude Aflame

In the heart's embrace, courage ignites,
Guided by faith, we soar to new heights.
With every step, grace lights the way,
A beacon of hope, in night and in day.

Strength from on high, in silence it flows,
In trials we stand, our spirit now grows.
Bound by love's thread, unwavering and true,
In the darkest of times, light breaks anew.

Whispers of the Almighty

In stillness we hear, soft voices profound,
Whispers of love, in the silence surround.
Trust in the path that the Spirit bestows,
A journey of grace, where the river flows.

Gentle the hand that guides us each day,
In moments of doubt, we find strength to stay.
With every heartbeat, the promise we claim,
United in purpose, we glorify His name.

The Sacred Strength Within

Deep in our souls, a wellspring of might,
A flicker of hope in the coldest of nights.
We rise from the ashes, renewed and alive,
In unity's grace, together we strive.

Belief is our armor, love is our sword,
In battles we face, we stand for the Lord.
With every challenge, we're never alone,
In faith's gentle whisper, our fears are outshone.

A Journey Through Trials

On roads paved with sorrow, we wander and seek,
Through valleys of shadow, we gather our strength.
In moments of struggle, our spirits unite,
Awakening courage, igniting the light.

With prayers like petals, we scatter our fears,
Sowing seeds of hope through the laughter and tears.
Hand in hand, we walk, through the storms that may come,
In the embrace of our faith, we have found our home.

The Light That Guides

In shadows deep, where echoes dwell,
A whisper calls, a silent bell.
The path is clear, the heart ignites,
In faith we walk, towards the lights.

With every step, the spirit lifts,
In trials faced, the soul receives.
Compassion spreads, like sunlit rays,
In unity, we share our days.

A beacon shines, through darkest night,
In weary hours, it brings us sight.
Together strong, we rise and sing,
Embracing love, our offering.

Through valleys low, and mountains tall,
In every struggle, we shall call.
For in His grace, we find our way,
The light that guides, both night and day.

Let faith be firm, as stars above,
In hearts entwined, we share His love.
With every breath, we seek the truth,
As children of the light, our youth.

A Symphony of Strength

In harmony, the voices rise,
A tapestry beneath the skies.
With every note, a sacred song,
In faith united, we belong.

Through stormy seas, we chart our course,
With steadfast hearts, and holy force.
In trials faced, our spirits soar,
Together strong, forevermore.

Each trial faced, a stepping stone,
In love's embrace, we're never alone.
With hands held high, we seek the light,
In every dark, we shine so bright.

In wisdom's heart, there lies our peace,
A gentle whisper, sweet release.
As faith is forged, in fires of grace,
We find our strength, embrace His face.

Through every tear, through every laugh,
A grand design, a sacred path.
In this great love, we shall prevail,
A symphony that will not fail.

Flames of the Spirit

In the silence of the night, we find,
A whispering blaze, so warm and kind.
Through trials fierce, the heart ignites,
With hope adorned, the soul takes flight.

Beneath the stars, our faith does shine,
With every tear, a sacred sign.
From ashes rise, the spirit's call,
In unity, we stand, we'll never fall.

A boon of grace, the fire spreads,
Through darkest paths, the light it leads.
With visions bright, our spirits soar,
Forever bound, forevermore.

Through storm and strife, our voices blend,
In prayerful song, we seek to mend.
For in this flame, our hearts align,
In love and strength, our lives entwine.

Together bright, we burn so fierce,
In joyful peace, our souls we pierce.
For in this dance, we find our way,
In flames of spirit, we shall stay.

A Covenant of Fortitude

In valleys deep, our roots hold strong,
A promise made where we belong.
With every step, we rise anew,
In faith we trust, the journey's true.

Through trials faced and fears embraced,
We gather courage, no time to waste.
In unity, our voices rise,
With hearts aflame, we reach the skies.

This covenant binds our hearts as one,
With every battle, victory's won.
With steadfast hearts and spirits bright,
We march together toward the light.

Though shadows loom and doubts may creep,
In sacred vows, our strength we keep.
With every heartbeat, we renew,
This sacred pact, we'll follow through.

In deep devotion, we shall stand,
In love's embrace, a gentle hand.
Together now, we reach the peak,
In fortitude, our spirits speak.

The Essence of Endurance

In the depths of night, our spirits gleam,
A flicker bright, a holy dream.
With breaths of hope, we carry on,
Through every storm, from dusk till dawn.

In trials faced, we find our way,
With grace to guide, we shall not sway.
In strength adorned, we rise anew,
The essence strong in all we do.

With weary hearts, yet bright and bold,
Our stories woven, truths retold.
Through every fall, we stand once more,
In love and faith, we shall restore.

In silence deep, we hear the call,
A gentle nudge that lifts us all.
Through pain and joy, our souls entwine,
In endurance pure, His love, divine.

Together bound, we shall prevail,
In every moment, love's holy tale.
For in the light of hope's embrace,
The essence of endurance finds its place.

Sacred Defiance

Through tempests wild, we stand awake,
With spirits fierce, no way to break.
In shadows cast, we'll hold our ground,
In sacred defiance, strength is found.

With hearts ablaze and voices strong,
We chase the echoes, heart and song.
Through trials harsh, we won't retreat,
In steadfast love, our faith's complete.

The path ahead may twist and turn,
Yet in our souls, the fire burns.
With every challenge, courage flows,
In unity, our spirit glows.

The world may falter, but we'll not fade,
In sacred trust, our bond is made.
Together we rise, unyielding, free,
In defiance sacred, we are three.

In the face of doubt, we shall rejoice,
For in our hearts, we've made a choice.
Together strong, we'll claim our prize,
In sacred defiance, our spirits rise.

Grace in Trials

In shadows deep, we seek the light,
Through storms we rise, our faith ignites.
The trials come, a testing ground,
In each heartache, grace is found.

With heavy burdens, we walk the road,
In weary moments, we share the load.
For every tear that falls like rain,
A whisper comes, it speaks our name.

In valleys low, we find our way,
His steadfast love, our guide each day.
When hope feels lost, He lifts us high,
With arms of mercy, we will fly.

So let us stand, though fears arise,
In prayers of faith, we lift our eyes.
For trials are but fleeting days,
In His embrace, we learn His ways.

The Rock of Ages

Upon the rock, we build our trust,
In Him alone, our hearts adjust.
Though winds may howl and waves may crash,
His love endures, a steadfast flash.

Through every storm, we cling to grace,
In trials fierce, we find our place.
With every doubt that clouds the mind,
His truth remains, a light defined.

The ages shift, yet He stands firm,
A solid hope, our hearts confirm.
In shadows deep, He will not sway,
For He's our guide, our night and day.

In silent nights when fears take hold,
The Rock of Ages, brave and bold.
With faith as strong as mountain peaks,
His gentle voice, our spirits speak.

Blessings in Burdens

In burdens borne, blessings unfold,
Through trials faced, our hearts grow bold.
Each heavy load, a chance to see,
The grace bestowed, the love set free.

For every struggle, wisdom gained,
In pain and sorrow, joy's not drained.
The seeds of hope in darkness sown,
Through humble paths, our strength is grown.

In silent trials, patience blooms,
As faith ignites, the spirit tunes.
With every tear, a story told,
Of love divine, of mercy bold.

So let us lift our hands in praise,
For burdens lend to brighter days.
In every cross, a crown awaits,
Through blessings found, our heart elates.

From Ashes to Ascendancy

From ashes cold, new life shall rise,
A phoenix formed, beneath the skies.
In brokenness, the soul takes flight,
From darkest nights to radiant light.

With each despair, the spirit learns,
In every trial, the flame still burns.
From dust and tears, we find our way,
Through stubborn hope, we greet the day.

The journey wrought with thorns and tears,
Yet beauty springs from countless fears.
In every fall, a chance to grow,
From ashes strewn, we reap and sow.

So rise again, with hearts renewed,
In every loss, a strength imbued.
From ashes to ascendancy,
In grace we walk, eternally.

Trusting Through Darkness

In shadows deep, I hear Your voice,
A whisper soft, I make my choice.
Through trials rough, my heart will stand,
Your guiding light, my steady hand.

Though storms may rage and doubts arise,
I lift my gaze, I seek the skies.
In every tear, a promise found,
Your grace abounds, my hope unbound.

With every step, You lead the way,
In darkest nights, You are my day.
Through faith I walk, in trust I soar,
Your love sustains, forevermore.

The Grit of Grace

In trials faced, I find my might,
With every fall, I learn to fight.
Your strength in me, a steadfast fire,
I rise anew, my heart's desire.

The path is steep, but grace is near,
In whispered prayers, You calm my fear.
Though bruised and worn, I stand upright,
With grit and grace, I seek the light.

The burdens bear, yet I stand tall,
For in Your love, I'll never fall.
With faith as armor, hope my guide,
In grit and grace, I will abide.

Threads of Hope

In woven strands, our lives entwined,
Your purpose clear, Your love defined.
Each moment shared, a sacred thread,
With every prayer, the heart is fed.

Through trials faced, the weave grows tight,
In darkest hours, I seek Your light.
Though shadows loom and doubts persist,
With threads of hope, I still resist.

Each stitch a blessing, gentle, free,
In tapestry of faith, I see.
A future bright, with love in scope,
We courageously sow, threads of hope.

Following the Call

A gentle tug upon my heart,
A beckoning that won't depart.
Through winding paths, Your voice I'll chase,
In every trial, I find Your grace.

Where courage falters, faith will rise,
With open heart, I seek the skies.
Though fear may creep and doubts may fall,
I step in trust, following the call.

With every step, You guide my way,
In shadows deep, You light the day.
In every challenge, I will strive,
For in Your love, I am alive.

Rising from Ashes

From ashes we rise, with hope aglow,
The spirit renewed, as faith will show.
In shadows of doubt, the light breaks through,
Rebirth from the trials, we start anew.

With every fall, a lesson learned,
In every sorrow, the heart has burned.
Embrace the struggle, let courage ignite,
For in brokenness, we find our might.

From the depths of despair, we shall climb,
Each step a prayer, each moment divine.
And though we stumble, we rise on the brink,
In unity with love, we shall not sink.

The Blessings of Adversity

In trials we find, the strength to grow,
Through storms we weather, our spirits flow.
What once felt heavy, now carries grace,
In adversity's clutch, we embrace our place.

The shadows may loom, but we press on,
Each struggle a spark, till the night is gone.
When walls close in, find faith as your key,
Unlocking the doors of possibility.

Through fiery trials, our souls are refined,
What's shattered and broken will be redefined.
For blessings lie deep in lessons of pain,
Emerging renewed, through the struggle we gain.

Voices of the Unseen

In silence they speak, the whispers are clear,
Voices of the unseen, urging us near.
Through darkness and doubt, their echoes resound,
In faith's gentle arms, we are unbound.

From valleys low, to mountains so high,
The unseen guide us, like stars in the sky.
Within every heart, their wisdom does dwell,
In the stillness we hear, their unspoken spell.

Through trials we face, their presence we feel,
In moments of doubt, their truth we reveal.
Let us listen closely, to the songs of the soul,
As together we journey, towards the ultimate goal.

A Covenant of Determination

In the covenant made, with each sacred vow,
We stand together, unwavering now.
Fueled by a fire, of purpose and grace,
In this walk of faith, we find our place.

No mountain too steep, no river too wide,
With love as our compass, we shall abide.
Through trials and tempests, we boldly declare,
A spirit unyielding, we rise from despair.

With hands intertwined, we nurture the dream,
In unity's strength, we're more than we seem.
For in every struggle, our bond will grow strong,
Together in faith, we will sing our song.

In the Embrace of Providence

In every shadow, grace does dwell,
A whisper soft, a sacred swell.
Through trials harsh, we find our way,
In providence, we choose to stay.

The stars above, they guide our fate,
With steadfast hands, we will not wait.
Each breath a prayer, each step a song,
In love's embrace, we all belong.

When darkness looms, and fears arise,
We lift our hearts toward starlit skies.
For in the storm, our spirits soar,
In faith we trust, forevermore.

Beneath the weight of worldly strife,
We seek the light that gives us life.
In gentle hands, our souls are cradled,
In grace's warmth, our hearts are railed.

So let us walk this path of grace,
Together bound, we find our place.
In unity, we sing as one,
In providence, our race is run.

The Weight of Glory

Upon the dawn, the light breaks free,
A gift of hope for all to see.
In every heart, the seeds we sow,
The weight of glory, ours to know.

With humble hands, we lift our eyes,
And seek the truth beyond the skies.
Through trials passed, we rise anew,
In love's embrace, we find our due.

The burdens carried, heavy yet bright,
Transform to wings that take our flight.
In faith, we find our purpose clear,
The weight of glory draws us near.

When shadows fall and doubts assail,
We raise our voices, we will not fail.
For in the darkness, hope ignites,
The light of glory shines in nights.

So let us walk this sacred road,
With every step, we share the load.
In unity, our spirits sing,
The weight of glory, we shall bring.

When Grace Shone Bright

In quiet moments, grace descends,
A gentle touch that love extends.
In every heart, a spark ignites,
When grace shines bright, all shadow fights.

Through trials faced and burdens borne,
We find the light that guides us, worn.
With every tear, a lesson learned,
In grace's arms, our hearts have turned.

The whispers soft, they call us near,
In moments still, we lose our fear.
For in the silence, truths unfold,
When grace shines bright, we'll be consoled.

So let us seek the path of peace,
With open hearts, our souls release.
In every heart, the light will rise,
When grace shines bright, we reach the skies.

Together bound, we share our song,
In grace's love, we will belong.
With every breath, we sing anew,
When grace shines bright, we are made true.

Climbing the Peaks of Hope

On rugged trails, we make our way,
With hearts aflame, we seek the day.
Each step we take, a leap of faith,
Climbing the peaks where hope awaits.

The winds may howl, the storms may roar,
Yet in our souls, we strive for more.
For every challenge, there's a way,
In hope's embrace, we find our stay.

The journey long, but spirits strong,
With every stride, we sing our song.
In unity, our vision clear,
Climbing the peaks, we persevere.

With eyes uplifted, we will find,
The treasures laid for heart and mind.
For in each climb, a lesson learned,
Climbing the peaks, our spirits burned.

So hand in hand, we rise as one,
In hope's bright light, our race is run.
Together rising, we shall cope,
Climbing the peaks of endless hope.

The Sacred Journey

In the valley of shadows, we tread,
With whispers of faith, our spirits spread.
Each step a prayer, each moment divine,
Guided by love, our hearts intertwine.

Mountains may rise, challenges unfold,
Yet in unity, our stories are told.
The path may be rough, with burdens to bear,
But hope is a compass, forever to share.

Stars light the night, a celestial guide,
In the silence of darkness, we do not hide.
For every doubt, a conviction will bloom,
In the garden of trials, we find our room.

Across the horizon, horizons expand,
Together we'll walk, hand in hand.
With faces uplifted, we lift our voice,
In the dance of creation, we rejoice.

At journey's end, we shall look back with grace,
Finding in hardship, a sacred embrace.
For the path that we walked, though steep it may be,
Is a testament written, for all to see.

Celestial Courage

In the heart of despair, a spark shall ignite,
A flame of conviction, burning so bright.
With courage as armor, we stand side by side,
In the face of the storm, we're no longer denied.

Each whispered prayer, a guide in the dark,
With shadows receding, we gather our spark.
The weight of the world may bend our resolve,
But faith is the force that helps us evolve.

As eagles we rise, above tempest and fear,
Our hearts filled with dreams, our vision is clear.
With wings of compassion, we soar to the sky,
In the arms of the Spirit, we learn how to fly.

Together we march, through valleys unknown,
With love as our ground, no one stands alone.
In the symphony of life, each note is a song,
With celestial courage, we know we belong.

When trials beset us, we call on the light,
Guided by faith, we embrace the fight.
In unity's strength, we shall always stand tall,
With celestial courage, we answer the call.

From Trials to Triumph

In the furnace of trials, our spirits are tried,
Yet in the ashes, resilience will bide.
Faith fuels the fire, hope shapes the mold,
From each bitter challenge, a victory unfolds.

Waves may be turbulent, and winds may assail,
But within our hearts, bravery prevails.
With purpose as anchor, we navigate seas,
Through storms of affliction, we find our peace.

Every setback's a lesson, a step on the way,
Towards triumph that beckons, come what may.
With whispers of courage stitched in each seam,
We'll face every obstacle, build every dream.

As rays of the sun paint the horizon gold,
Stories of conquest are lovingly told.
From trials to triumph, a journey we share,
In the embrace of the Spirit, we find strength to dare.

In the dance of our lives, we rise and we sway,
From shadows of doubt into the new day.
With hearts intertwined, we'll carry the light,
From trials to triumph, we'll shine ever bright.

The Light of Endurance

Through valleys of pain, we journey on still,
With the light of endurance, we bend but won't chill.
Each tear is a testimony, a tale of the soul,
Forging endurance, making us whole.

In the silence of nights, when darkness creeps near,
We gather our faith, transforming the fear.
The dawn of tomorrow brings hope to our sight,
With the light of endurance, we rise with the light.

Mountains may crumble, and rivers may dry,
But with love in our hearts, we will not comply.
For the strength of our spirit, like an endless sea,
Is the light of endurance, setting us free.

As paths may diverge, and journeys may part,
We walk on united, our strength is our heart.
Through trials we wander, through pain we advance,
In the light of endurance, we forever dance.

In the end, it's the journey that shapes who we are,
A canvas of struggle, with hope as a star.
Through shadows and storms, we've learned to endure,
With the light of endurance, our spirits are pure.

The Heart of a Believer

In quiet prayer, the soul does rise,
A flicker of faith in weary skies.
With humble heart and open mind,
A path of grace we hope to find.

For in the whispers, truth shall dwell,
In every heartache, love will swell.
Through trials faced, the spirit grows,
In every tear, God's promise flows.

The sacred light within us glows,
Embracing all, as mercy shows.
With every breath, we seek His will,
In quiet moments, faith does fill.

Through every storm, His strength we claim,
In darkest nights, we call His name.
Together bound, we lift our praise,
In unity, our hearts ablaze.

The heart of a believer beats,
In joyful hymns, our spirit meets.
With hands uplifted, we rejoice,
In every moment, we find our voice.

From Weakness to Valor

In shadows deep, where doubts reside,
A flicker sparks, we turn the tide.
From broken dreams, our faith ignites,
To face the battles, reach new heights.

With trembling hands, we rise to fight,
Embracing truth, we seek the light.
In every struggle, courage grows,
As Heart of the Savior gently shows.

From weakness found, a warrior's heart,
Grace transforms, we play our part.
Together strong, we heed the call,
In every stumble, we stand tall.

With every prayer, a shield we bear,
In trials faced, He proves His care.
Through valleys low, we press ahead,
In strength renewed, our spirits fed.

From weakness blooms a glorious tale,
In faith and hope, we shall not fail.
With valor's shield, and courage's sword,
We rise as one, proclaiming the Lord.

Wings of the Spirit

Upon the winds, our spirits soar,
In sacred flight, we seek for more.
With every prayer, we lift our soul,
In love divine, we find our goal.

The burdens lift as hearts take wing,
In praise and worship, we shall sing.
With every whisper, hope entwined,
The wings of faith, our hearts aligned.

To touch the sky, to be set free,
In spirit's dance, a symphony.
With grace bestowed, we rise anew,
A promise held, forever true.

In stillness deep, the truth we find,
A gentle breeze, the ties that bind.
Each step we take, He leads us on,
Through trials faced, His light is dawn.

So let us soar with spirits high,
In every dream, we learn to fly.
With faith unfurled, our spirits bright,
In joy and peace, we find our light.

The Power of the Redeemed

In grace bestowed, our chains are gone,
The power of love, our hearts live on.
With every sin, His mercy flows,
In redemption's light, true freedom grows.

From ashes raised, we are made whole,
In open arms, He heals the soul.
No shadow dark can take away,
The light of hope, our guiding ray.

With hearts awakened, we take our stand,
In faith united, hand in hand.
The power of the redeemed we share,
With every soul, we show we care.

Through storms of life, the battles fought,
In every lesson, wisdom taught.
Our voices rise, in one accord,
Together singing, praise of the Lord.

The power of love, a flame that burns,
In every heart, a passion churns.
For in our flaws, His strength revealed,
The power of the redeemed is sealed.

Shielded by Belief

In the shadow of doubt, we find light,
A faith that ignites the darkest night.
With prayer as our shield, we stand tall,
In unity, we answer the sacred call.

When storms rage fierce, and fears take flight,
We seek the truth, bathed in pure light.
Together we walk, hand in hand,
In the garden of hope, we take our stand.

Each tear a prayer, each sigh a song,
With hearts aligned, we grow strong.
Through trials faced, we rise above,
In the arms of grace, we feel His love.

Bound by a promise, we journey forth,
In the heart of faith, we find our worth.
With every whisper, a guiding beam,
In the embrace of belief, we dream.

So let not fear cast shadows deep,
For in His presence, our spirits leap.
Shielded by belief, we will prevail,
In His divine light, we shall not fail.

Rise Like Eagles

When mountains loom and valleys dip low,
We lift our gaze, the truth we know.
With wings of faith, we soar the skies,
In the strength of peace, our spirit flies.

Through trials faced and paths unclear,
We find our courage, we have no fear.
Like eagles strong, we rise with grace,
In the arms of hope, we find our place.

With every storm, a lesson learned,
From ashes rise, our hearts now burned.
Together we climb, reaching for light,
In the warmth of love, we take flight.

With eyes set high, we chase our dreams,
In the tapestry of faith, we weave seams.
United in purpose, we chase the call,
Together as one, we shall not fall.

So let us rise, like eagles bold,
Embrace the journey, the stories told.
With faith as our guide, together we'll soar,
In the spirit of love, forevermore.

Harvest of Tenacity

In fields of trials, where seeds are sown,
We cultivate strength, from heart to bone.
With hands that labor, and spirits bright,
We reap the harvest, through darkest night.

Each struggle faced, a lesson learned,
In the fires of life, our passion burned.
With tenacity strong, we push ahead,
In the garden of faith, we are fed.

Through seasons of doubt, we stand so true,
With every challenge, we break anew.
In unity's bond, we find our way,
The fruits of our labor shining each day.

With gratitude's heart, we give and share,
In the echo of hope, we find our prayer.
Harvesting joy, in every stride,
In the name of love, let us abide.

So let us gather, the fruits of our toil,
In the sanctuary of faith, we shall not spoil.
For with each seed, a promise we see,
In the harvest of tenacity, we are free.

The Sanctuary of Courage

In the stillness of night, our hearts ignite,
A sanctuary built from faith and light.
In shadows cast, we find our way,
With courage leading, we shall not sway.

Through valleys of fear, with spirits bold,
We share our stories, the truth unfolds.
In the face of doubt, we raise our voice,
In unity's strength, we make a choice.

Hand in hand, we lift each other,
In the embrace of love, we find our brother.
For in this space, we stand as one,
In the sanctuary of courage, we've begun.

Let not the storms define our fate,
With hearts ablaze, we shall not wait.
For every step taken together here,
We build a legacy, strong and clear.

So let us rise, inspired and free,
In the sanctuary of courage, we shall be.
With faith as our armor, hope as our guide,
Together in love, we shall abide.

The Testament of the Brave

In shadows deep, where courage hides,
They forged their path, where faith abides.
With steadfast hearts and spirits bold,
Their stories of valor, forever told.

Through storms and trials, they stand true,
In the light of grace, their strength renew.
They rise again, when hope is thin,
For in their hearts, the spirit's kin.

With angels near and whispers clear,
They tread the path, casting out fear.
In every struggle, in every fight,
They shine like stars, through darkest night.

Their hands uplifted in prayerful plea,
Claiming the promise, the victory.
Through sweat and tears, they find their way,
In the testament of night and day.

And as they march, with heads held high,
They touch the sky, their spirits fly.
For the brave shall rise, as angels favor,
In the saga of love, forever savored.

Pillars of Perseverance

In the temple of time, they stand so tall,
Strong in their faith, they heed the call.
Through trials grim, they find their grace,
With enduring love, they seek His face.

Each heavy stone, a tale untold,
With patient hearts, they break the mold.
They gather strength, not from their own,
But from the seeds of faith they've sown.

Through fire and rain, they stand their ground,
In every struggle, His love is found.
Their spirits soar where hope should wane,
For in their trials, they find His name.

O, pillars strong, of hope and light,
They turn to Him, to seek the right.
In every journey, in every climb,
They walk with purpose, transcending time.

With each new dawn, their hearts unite,
Together in love, they shine so bright.
For every step, they pave the way,
The pillars of faith, come what may.

The Blessing of Trials

In moments of doubt, the soul will yearn,
To find the light, in darkness discern.
For every trial, a blessing unfolds,
In the heart's embrace, the truth is told.

Through valleys low, they learn to rise,
Glimpses of grace, in tear-streaked eyes.
Each challenge faced, a lesson learned,
With every step, the flame has burned.

With hands outstretched, they seek the path,
Embracing His love, through joy and wrath.
For in the depths, the spirit grows,
And in the pain, His comfort flows.

The blessings come, not dressed in gold,
But in the stories of courage bold.
In trials faced, their hearts will sing,
Of the joy and peace His presence brings.

So let them dance, through each despair,
For every test, draws them to prayer.
In the embrace of trials, they find grace,
As blessings bloom in the darkest space.

Heavens' Steadfast

Beyond the stars, where silence reigns,
The heavens call, through joys and pains.
In every heartbeat, their love sustains,
A steady light, in life's constraints.

When storms arise, and fears collide,
They whisper hope, when hearts divide.
For every soul that seeks the sun,
In heavenly arms, they are not alone.

With faith as anchor, they stand so strong,
Turning to Him, where they belong.
In ancient texts, the truths abide,
Heaven's steadfast, their faithful guide.

Each prayer ascends, like fragrant flow'rs,
To touch the skies, in sacred hours.
In stillness found, their spirits soar,
For heaven's steadfast, they long for more.

Through trials faced, they hold on tight,
With eyes fixed high, they choose the light.
For in the journey, through joy and strife,
Heaven's embrace, the essence of life.

Altar of Determination

Upon the stone, my vow I lay,
With fervent heart, I rise to pray.
Each trial faced, each heavy load,
A burning faith, my spirit's ode.

In shadows deep, I find the light,
A guiding star, my soul's delight.
With every step, I forge my path,
The power blooms in love, not wrath.

Resilience grows in storms I brace,
In every tear, I see His grace.
Unyielding strength, a holy gift,
No mountain high can cause a rift.

Upon this altar, dreams reside,
With every challenge, hope's my guide.
Through faith and toil, I stand renewed,
In sacred trust, my life imbued.

The Ladder of Belief

A ladder built with trust and dreams,
Each rung ascends, a light that beams.
To heaven's gate, my spirit climbs,
With whispered prayers in sacred rhymes.

In every doubt, a step is made,
The fabric of my faith displayed.
Through trials vast, my heart will soar,
Each challenge met opens new door.

With every heartbeat, courage found,
In quiet moments, grace surrounds.
The climb is steep, but I remain,
With love and truth, I break the chain.

Divine assistance guides my way,
In darkest nights, I see the day.
My spirit rises, fierce and free,
Belief transforms what's meant to be.

Divine Endurance

In trials faced, let strength arise,
The heavens watch, the angels sigh.
Through every storm, I find my core,
With faith, I march forevermore.

When weary bones begin to ache,
A warmth within, the dawn will break.
Each breath a prayer, each goal a song,
In sacred whispers, I belong.

With steadfast heart, I brave the night,
Thy love, my armor, pure and bright.
With every heartbeat, I'm reborn,
In trials fierce, my soul is worn.

Resilience flows through every vein,
In darkest moments, I'll remain.
For in this journey, I am blessed,
To bear the weight with holy rest.

The Shield of Providence

A shield of grace, I hold it high,
Through life's fierce storms, my faith draws nigh.
In shadows cast, I find my peace,
With every doubt, my courage cease.

In paths unknown, His hand I seek,
In silent prayers, my spirit speaks.
Protection surrounds from skies above,
In every trial, I feel His love.

Secure within this sacred trust,
With every fear, I rise from dust.
The trials faced become my song,
In sacred union, I belong.

Through valleys low and mountains tall,
I rise adorned by heaven's call.
With every heartbeat, truth asserts,
This shield of faith, my heart converts.

Faithful Fortitude

In shadows deep, we find our way,
Guided by light, through night to day.
With steadfast hearts, we boldly stand,
United in faith, hand in hand.

Through trials fierce, our spirits soar,
With every storm, we seek for more.
A sacred bond that cannot break,
For in our souls, true strength we make.

The path is long, yet hope is bright,
In darkest hours, we cling to light.
Each struggle faced, a lesson learned,
In faith's embrace, our hearts are turned.

With faith as shield, we face the day,
Through every doubt, we find our way.
In whispered prayers, our courage grows,
For in His name, our spirit knows.

So stand we firm, with hearts ablaze,
In faithful steps, we sing His praise.
For fortitude in every breath,
Awakens life, defies all death.

Resilience of the Spirit

When storms do rise and shadows creep,
The spirit's will is ours to keep.
In silence loud, our voices clear,
We rise again, casting aside fear.

In every trial, a seed is sown,
In fertile ground, our faith has grown.
With every struggle, strength is gained,
A tapestry of hope is framed.

The spirit weaves its purest thread,
In moments bleak, its light is spread.
Through every wound, we heal and mend,
For in our hearts, His love transcends.

In gentle breaths, we seek His grace,
With open hands, we find our place.
Resilience flows, a river wide,
In trust and love, we shall abide.

With spirits high, we face each plight,
The dawn shall come, dispelling night.
With every heartbeat, we draw near,
In resilience, we have no fear.

The Armor of Belief

In battles fought, our armor gleams,
Each piece a truth, a hope that beams.
In faith we trust, our hearts intact,
With love as shield, no fear to act.

The helm of peace upon our brow,
The sword of truth, we wield it now.
In troubled times, we stand our ground,
With courage fierce, our souls unbound.

With every foe that seeks to sway,
Our armor holds, we will not stray.
In unity, our voices rise,
A chorus strong that never dies.

In faith, we fortify our might,
With trust in Him, we face the fight.
For every tear has forged our way,
In battles won, we learn to pray.

So wear your armor, stand with pride,
In belief's embrace, we will abide.
With every heartbeat, strong and free,
In His protection, we shall be.

The Unyielding Heart

In silence speaks the unyielding heart,
A flame of faith that won't depart.
Through trials fierce, it beats anew,
With love and hope, it sees us through.

Each wound a mark of strength bestowed,
In life's great journey, love has flowed.
With every breath, we rise again,
In unyielding grace, we will not bend.

The heart, a fortress, strong and true,
In every storm, it guides us through.
With whispers soft, divine embrace,
In unyielding love, we find our place.

With every heartbeat, courage blooms,
In darkest nights, hope brightly looms.
The unyielding heart, a beacon bright,
In faith's embrace, we find our light.

So carry on with hearts aflame,
In love's great echo, we speak His name.
For in the steadfastness we find,
The unyielding heart, forever kind.

A Journey Through Shadows

In darkness deep, where whispers dwell,
A path unfolds, a tale to tell.
Each step ignites a flickering light,
Guiding souls through the night.

With faith as shield, and hope as guide,
Through valleys low, we shall not hide.
Hand in hand, we face our fears,
For love transcends the flow of tears.

The shadows loom, yet faith remains,
Through trials faced, our courage gains.
In every heart, a spark divine,
Awakens strength in the design.

Embrace the dawn, let shadows part,
In unity, we forge our art.
Together we rise, a radiant chorus,
In the embrace of love, we find our solace.

So onward we tread, with hearts aglow,
Through every storm, we learn, we grow.
In the journey through shadows, we find grace,
For in the darkness, we seek His face.

Alchemy of Faith

In humble hearts, a seed is sown,
Through trials faced, our spirits grown.
The alchemy of faith begins,
Transforming loss to holy wins.

Through fire and flame, our souls are forged,
In patience brewed, our hearts enlarged.
What once was pain, now turns to gold,
A witness to the dreams unfold.

Each prayer a potion, crafted fine,
With trust, we stir the sacred wine.
In unity, our voices rise,
A symphony beneath the skies.

The journey twists, the path may sway,
Yet grace will guide us, come what may.
In every heart, a sacred space,
The alchemy of faith, our timeless grace.

So let us walk, in love entwined,
The treasures found, in hope aligned.
With every step, our spirits soar,
In the alchemy of faith, forevermore.

The Triumph of Grace

In shadows cast, where doubts reside,
A gentle voice, our hearts abide.
The triumph of grace, our steadfast theme,
Awakens hope, ignites the dream.

With every fall, we rise anew,
In trials faced, our strength shines through.
The past may haunt like ghostly chains,
Yet grace unbinds and love remains.

Each tear we shed, a story told,
Of faith restored and hearts consoled.
In every struggle, victory waits,
For grace surrounds, and love debaits.

With open hearts, we find the way,
In every night, comes the day.
United strong, we sing His praise,
In the triumph of grace, our souls ablaze.

So let us dance, rejoice, and sing,
For in our weakness, grace takes wing.
In every moment, sweet embrace,
We find our peace in the triumph of grace.

In the Hands of Providence

In quiet moments, still and bright,
We seek the hand that guides our sight.
In the hands of providence, we rest,
Trusting the journey, we are blessed.

With every breath, His plan unfolds,
Through trials faced, His love enfolds.
In whispered prayers, our hearts align,
In the hands of providence, we shine.

Though paths may twist and shadows fall,
We stand together, answering the call.
For every challenge faced in grace,
In the hands of providence, we find our place.

With open arms, we face the day,
In trust we walk, come what may.
Guided by love, we find our way,
In the hands of providence, we choose to stay.

So let us cherish, every phase,
In gratitude, we sing His praise.
In every heartbeat, His love we sense,
Forever held in providence.

A Tapestry of Triumph

In shadows deep, where hope may fade,
A light breaks forth, the dawn arrayed.
With hearts uplifted, we rise as one,
In faith adorned, our battles won.

Each thread of love, a story spun,
Through trials faced, the victory's begun.
Hand in hand, we walk the way,
With grace bestowed, come what may.

In every tear, a promise sown,
In every trial, our strength is grown.
The tapestry we weave with care,
Is stitched with prayers, a sacred flare.

Through storms we march, our spirits bold,
In unity's embrace, our hearts unfold.
With voices raised, we sing our song,
In triumph sweet, we all belong.

For love prevails through darkest night,
In every heart, a spark ignites.
With gratitude, we lift our eyes,
A tapestry of triumph, 'neath endless skies.

The Path of Unwavering Trust

Upon the road where whispers dwell,
In every step, we feel Him swell.
With faith our guide, and hope our light,
The path unfolds, a blessed sight.

Through valleys low and mountains high,
In quiet faith, we learn to fly.
For every trial, a lesson shared,
In love's embrace, we know we're cared.

With open hearts, we tread the way,
Through shadows deep, into the day.
In every struggle, trust takes root,
In humble hearts, our faith bears fruit.

Though storms may rage, we stand secure,
With unwavering trust, our path is sure.
In every moment, we find His grace,
In every heartbeat, His warm embrace.

And when the night brings doubt and fear,
We hold to love, His voice so near.
For on this path, we walk with light,
In unwavering trust, we find our might.

Embracing the Divine Will

In silent prayer, we seek His face,
With open hearts, we find our place.
Through trials vast, our spirits soar,
In every heartbeat, we feel Him more.

With gentle hands, He molds our fate,
In every moment, we learn to wait.
For His design, so pure and bright,
Guides us onward, into the light.

As seasons change, and rivers flow,
In trusting grace, our spirits grow.
Embracing all the paths He shows,
With faith steadfast, our love just glows.

With courage held, we face the day,
In surrender sweet, we find our way.
For in His will, our hearts align,
In every whisper, we see the divine.

So let us walk with open hearts,
In every challenge, find new starts.
Embracing His will, we find our peace,
Through love eternal, our joys increase.

Lifting the Veil of Doubt

Amidst the fog, where shadows play,
We lift the veil, embracing the day.
With weary souls, we yearn for light,
In faith, we rise, our spirits bright.

For doubt may whisper, tempt us near,
Yet love's soft voice, we hold so dear.
In every trial, we find the grace,
To persevere, in this sacred space.

With hands outstretched, we seek the truth,
In every moment, reborn in youth.
For through the darkness, we shall see,
The light of faith will set us free.

Together we stand, hearts intertwined,
In unity's strength, our paths aligned.
Where doubts are quenched, and fears take flight,
We lift the veil, embracing the light.

And as we walk this journey wide,
With open hearts, let love abide.
In lifting doubt, we find our song,
In harmony, we all belong.

Pillars of Grace

In the stillness of dawn's light,
We seek Your grace, oh Divine,
With hearts wide open in flight,
Your love is the path we find.

Through trials our faith shall grow,
In shadows, Your light we trace,
With each step, our spirits glow,
Together we stand in grace.

Every burden, You shall bear,
With wisdom our guiding star,
In Your arms, we find repair,
Your whispers, a soothing scar.

The winds of change how they blow,
Yet our hearts in rhythm hum,
In the depths, where rivers flow,
Tides of hope shall always come.

With the strength of mountain peaks,
We rise above, hand in hand,
In unity, our heart speaks,
In faith, we forever stand.

A Prayer for Perseverance

In darkness we raise our plea,
Grant us courage, be our guide,
Through the storms, may we be free,
In Your strength, we shall abide.

When the journey feels too long,
And our footsteps start to wane,
Let Your wisdom be our song,
In the struggle, ease our pain.

With each challenge that we face,
Fill our hearts with hope anew,
In the trials, show Your grace,
Let us feel Your presence true.

As we walk this path of light,
Every step a sacred vow,
In Your love, we find our fight,
With Your peace, we conquer now.

Though the night may seem so vast,
Trust in You, our guiding flame,
In our hearts, Your love holds fast,
In Your name, we spread our claim.

Echoes of Courage

In the silence of the night,
We hear whispers, soft and clear,
Voices of those who've taken flight,
In Your grace, we lose our fear.

Through the valleys deep and wide,
Brave the storms, oh Lord, we stand,
With each echo, faith our guide,
In this journey, hand in hand.

Let the trials come, we pray,
For in struggle, strength is born,
As the dawn begins to sway,
In the light, our hopes are worn.

Each heartbeat sings of Your name,
In the courage, we shall bloom,
Through the fire, never the same,
In Your love, our fears consume.

With each step, we rise anew,
In the echoes, truth revealed,
Let our hearts be brave and true,
In Your love, our fate is sealed.

Divine Resilience

In the trials, strength appears,
With each moment, grace unfolds,
Casting away our earthly fears,
In Your warmth, our spirit holds.

Though the path may twist and turn,
With steadfast hearts, we endure,
In the lessons, wisdom's earned,
Each struggle, a call to cure.

Let the storms rage on about,
In Your shelter, we find peace,
With every doubt, we'll rise, no doubt,
In Your mercy, fears release.

Through the shadows, we shall tread,
Hand in hand, through thick and thin,
In Your promise, hopes are fed,
With each breath, we shall begin.

May our journey, bold and bright,
Reflect the strength of Your embrace,
In this world, we share the light,
Together, we seek Your face.

The Sound of an Unbroken Will

In the silence, strength does grow,
With faith as our guiding light,
Whispers of hope, they softly flow,
In storms of doubt, we hold on tight.

Every trial, a step to take,
Shadows loom, yet we stand firm,
A heart ignited, no fear to break,
In love's embrace, we shall affirm.

Boundless spirit rising high,
Echoes of promises we hear,
With each breath, we touch the sky,
A symphony of joy, sincere.

Through the darkness, we will tread,
An unbroken will, our steady sail,
With every heartbeat, love is spread,
In unity, we shall prevail.

Fountains of Inner Power

Deep within, a fountain flows,
Whispers of strength, divine and pure,
In quiet moments, truth bestows,
A well of peace, steadfast and sure.

Mountains rise, yet we are free,
Flowing rivers, grace unconfined,
Within our souls, the key we see,
In the stillness, hope aligned.

Wellspring of wisdom, age-old truth,
By nurturing faith, we ignite the spark,
In vibrant joy, we find our youth,
Illuminated paths in the dark.

From depths of prayer, we rise anew,
Empowered hearts, with courage blessed,
Fountains of grace, eternal and true,
In love's embrace, we find our rest.

Chosen for the Challenge

In every struggle, purpose shines,
A call to arms in faith's embrace,
With hearts aligned, our spirit twines,
To face the trials with steadfast grace.

Each burden borne, a lesson learned,
Through valleys low and mountains steep,
In fiery trials, our souls are turned,
To uncover treasures, ours to keep.

Chosen souls for battles great,
With strength bestowed from worlds above,
In shadows cast, we align our fate,
Through unity, we rise in love.

In whispers fierce, our mission clear,
Together we stand, unbowed by fear,
Embracing challenges, we hold dear,
For in each moment, truth appears.

In the Presence of the Infinite

Beneath the stars, in twilight's glow,
We seek the presence, pure and grand,
In quiet awe, our spirits flow,
In the infinite, we take our stand.

Eternity whispers in gentle tones,
With every heartbeat, we align,
In sacred space, a truth condones,
Love's boundless reach, forever entwined.

In the stillness, we are found,
The universe pulses, alive and whole,
In reverence deep, our hearts resound,
Bound by the thread, the cosmic soul.

In the presence of awe and grace,
We embrace the light that shows the way,
Together as one, we find our place,
In infinite love, forever stay.

The Armor of Faith

In trials fierce, we stand in grace,
Our faith, a shield in every place.
With prayers that rise, like incense sweet,
We find our strength, we stand on our feet.

Clad in truth, our souls are bright,
With love and hope, we face the night.
Each scripture vast, a guiding star,
In darkest hours, we know where we are.

Honor the vows that bind our fate,
For in the storm, we shall not wait.
The light within, our constant flame,
In unity, we praise His name.

With hearts ablaze, we march ahead,
In every word, our spirits fed.
The armor strong, it bears the test,
In faith we find our truest rest.

Together bound, we shall not break,
With every trial, we shall awake.
For in His love, we find our way,
The Armor of Faith, our guiding ray.

Echoes of Resilience

From depths of despair, we rise anew,
In whispers soft, the truth shines through.
Each struggle faced, a lesson gained,
In silent strength, our hearts unchained.

Through shadows cast, we stand as one,
In unity forged, our battles won.
In tears and trials, our spirits grew,
With hope renewed, we start anew.

The echoes ring from ages past,
A legacy of love to last.
With every breath, we carry on,
In faith and courage, we are strong.

Through every doubt, we shall persist,
In prayerful hearts, we shall not miss.
For in the darkest times we see,
The echoes call, "You're meant to be."

With every step, we claim our place,
In grace we walk, our fears we face.
Resilience born from trials met,
In sacred light, we won't forget.

Pillars of My Spirit

The pillars rise, a steadfast beam,
Faith and hope, forever gleam.
In every heartbeat, strength resides,
In sacred trust, our spirit guides.

With visions clear, we seek the light,
In darkest hours, we find our might.
For gratitude, the ground we stand,
In every prayer, a gentle hand.

The pillars firm, they won't be swayed,
In trials faced, in love displayed.
United hearts, we forge ahead,
By His great promise, we are led.

In silent moments, we listen close,
To whispers soft that grant us hope.
The pillars strong, they bear our weight,
In divine love, we celebrate.

With every dawn, we rise with grace,
These pillars hold, our sacred space.
Together we build, in faith we stand,
Pillars of spirit, hand in hand.

The Unyielding Heart

With every trial that comes our way,
The unyielding heart shall surely stay.
In love's embrace, we find our fire,
A strength that burns, a deep desire.

Through storms that roar and shadows cast,
We hold our ground, we stand steadfast.
In faith we rise, through pain and fear,
The voice of hope, for all to hear.

Each heartbeat echoes, truth's decree,
An unyielding heart shall always be.
In gentle whispers, we find our peace,
A promise kept, our souls release.

Resilience blooms from roots so deep,
In every challenge, we shall leap.
With courage strong, we face the fight,
The unyielding heart ignites the light.

For love endures, we shall not break,
In every moment, our vows we make.
With open arms, we meet the day,
The unyielding heart, our steadfast way.

Navigating the Wilderness

In shadows deep, where echoes dwell,
Faith guides our steps, a whispered spell.
The path is rough, the night is long,
Yet in our hearts, we carry song.

With every trial, our spirits soar,
Through barren land, He opens door.
His light a beacon, warm and bright,
In darkest hours, He brings the light.

The trees may sway, the winds may moan,
But in His grace, we're never alone.
Our voices rise, a hymn of hope,
With faith as anchor, we learn to cope.

Each stone we tread, a story told,
Of burdens shared and hands to hold.
In wilderness, we seek His face,
Finding our way, embraced by grace.

So here we stand, with hearts aglow,
Through trials faced, our spirits grow.
With every step in faith, we trust,
In wilderness, our hearts adjust.

The Test of the True Believer

When shadows loom and doubts arise,
The heart must beat, and the spirit tries.
In silence deep, we feel the weight,
Yet through the pain, we cultivate.

Hands lifted high amid the storm,
Strengthened by grace, a sacred norm.
With every tear that graces cheek,
A truth emerges, and hearts grow meek.

For in the test, our faith is forged,
Like gold refined, from trials we emerge.
Each challenge met with courage bright,
An ember glows, igniting light.

In darkest hours, His presence near,
A whispered promise, "Do not fear."
As we surrender to His plan,
The path unfurls, and we shall stand.

Through valleys low and mountains high,
The true believer learns to fly.
His love our guide, forever true,
In every breath, we're made anew.

Radiance Through Tribulations

In trials faced, our spirits bleed,
Yet from the pain, we cultivate seed.
The radiance born from darkest night,
Bears witness to His boundless light.

With every wound, a lesson learned,
Through every heartache, our souls discerned.
In moments bleak, His love prevails,
A calming force when faith entails.

We rise from ashes, renewed and strong,
With every trial, we find our song.
The light within begins to shine,
Reflecting truth, forever divine.

Each step we take in faith and grace,
Illuminates our sacred space.
For in the struggle, beauty grows,
Resilient hearts, where radiance glows.

So let us walk through fire's embrace,
With hope unyielding, we find our place.
Through tribulations, love ignites,
Our spirits soar on heaven's heights.

Stones of Faithful Foundation

Each stone we gather tells a tale,
Of trials faced and moments frail.
Through faith and love, we build our home,
In unity, we are never alone.

A foundation laid on promises kept,
In our hearts, the memories slept.
With courage strong, we stack them high,
A testament to the reasons why.

For every stone, a lesson learned,
Through faith unyielding, our hearts have turned.
Together we rise, a sturdy wall,
In His embrace, we shall not fall.

As life storms rage and winds may howl,
Our faithful hearts will never grow foul.
With love as our mortar, binding tight,
We stand together, a radiant light.

So let the world throw rocks our way,
We'll build our faith, come what may.
With every stone, we lift the past,
A foundation strong, forever to last.

The Strength Within

In the silence, faith will rise,
Whispers of truth beneath the skies.
With trust in heart, we face the day,
For hope's embrace shall lead the way.

Through trials deep, our spirits stand,
Guided by grace, divinely planned.
In every storm, His love we see,
Strengthening the soul, setting it free.

Mountains tremble, yet we remain,
Anchored in love that knows no pain.
With courage born from faith's embrace,
We rise anew, in sacred space.

Each breath a prayer, each step a choice,
In sacred silence, we find our voice.
The strength within, a holy flame,
In trials faced, we praise His name.

So let us walk this path of light,
With hearts united, ever bright.
In every shadow, grace shall flow,
The strength within, our souls shall grow.

Sanctified Will

In the quiet of our yearning hearts,
A whisper calls as the spirit imparts.
With every breath, we seek to know,
The sanctified will, in love it grows.

Through wandering paths, we find our way,
Guided by hope, come what may.
The sacred truth, it shines so clear,
In every moment, we draw Him near.

With open hands and yielded soul,
We surrender to a greater whole.
In trials faced, we look above,
For in our hearts, we sow His love.

Each lesson learned, a gift bestowed,
In sanctified will, our spirits glowed.
With faith unyielding, we shall stand,
In grace and mercy, hand in hand.

So let us trust the path we tread,
With every word and prayer we said.
The sanctified will, forever true,
In love's embrace, we are made new.

The Light of Tenacity

In the darkest night, a flame we find,
The light of tenacity guides the mind.
With every challenge, we rise and fight,
For deep within, we hold the light.

Through every trial, we shall not yield,
With hearts ignited, we take the field.
With faith our armor, love our sword,
Marching onward, we heed His word.

Each step we take, a testament true,
The light of tenacity breaks on through.
In every struggle, strength is born,
A sacred promise, the spirit's dawn.

So let us hold the torch so bright,
With gratitude, we spread the light.
For in the journey, we come to see,
The light of tenacity sets us free.

In every heart, the fire's aglow,
Through love and faith, together we grow.
The light of tenacity shines within,
Eternal hope, our sacred hymn.

Cherished Foundations

In every heart lies cherished ground,
Where seeds of hope and love abound.
Built on faith, a sturdy base,
In every moment, we seek His grace.

Through trials faced, our roots grow deep,
In cherished foundations, truths we keep.
With every prayer, we nurture soil,
In love's embrace, our spirits toil.

So let us tend to what we sow,
With kindness, mercy, let it flow.
For in the heart where love resides,
Cherished foundations, hope abides.

In every heart, a spark ignites,
Illuminating our darkest nights.
With faith as our anchor, we shall stand,
Cherished foundations, forever grand.

Together we build, together we grow,
With love as the compass, it always shows.
In cherished foundations, we rise and shine,
In every moment, His love divine.

Pillars of the Faithful

In shadows deep, they stand so strong,
Guiding hearts where they belong.
Roots in grace, they reach above,
Holding fast to hope and love.

With every prayer, the spirit soars,
Through trials faced, the heart implores.
Unity binds, like threads of light,
In darkest nights, they shine so bright.

Among the faithful, wisdom grows,
In whispered truths, the silence flows.
Together, we walk this sacred path,
With reverence, we escape the wrath.

Through storms and strife, they persevere,
In every doubt, their faith is clear.
With open arms, they bless the day,
As love unfolds, they gently sway.

In every heart, a sacred flame,
With courage vast, they seek His name.
Pillars of strength, forever true,
In every step, a life renewed.

Beneath the Divine Ceiling

In humble prayer, we softly kneel,
Beneath the arches, faith we feel.
Whispers of love fill the sacred space,
Hope ignites in every trace.

The sunlight streams through stained glass bright,
Casting colors of holy light.
With every breath, the spirit sings,
Embracing all that His mercy brings.

In unity, our voices raise,
Celebrating the divine praise.
With trust in hearts, our worries cease,
Finding solace, joy, and peace.

Beneath the ceiling, dreams take flight,
In every prayer, there shines the light.
Together we stand, hands intertwined,
A tapestry of souls combined.

In reverence, we gather near,
And share the love that casts out fear.
Beneath the roof of grace we see,
A glimpse of what we're meant to be.

Echoes of Strength

From mountains high, the echoes call,
In quiet strength, we rise, not fall.
Hearts united in common fight,
Guided by faith, our spirits bright.

With every trial, we grow anew,
In moments of doubt, His love shines through.
Together we stand, hand in hand,
With hope as our guide, we take a stand.

In silence, we listen, the whispers flow,
The strength of our bond begins to grow.
Through darkest nights, His promise stays,
Illuminating our tangled ways.

Echoes of courage, reverberate strong,
In togetherness, we belong.
With every heartbeat, we find our way,
In the light of dawn, we greet the day.

In each other's eyes, the truth we see,
Echoes of strength, forever free.
With faith as our fortress, we will endure,
In every storm, we will be secure.

Transcending Tribulation

Through trials faced, we hold the line,
In shadows thick, His light does shine.
With strength unyielding, we rise above,
Empowered by the grace of love.

In every burden, a lesson lies,
Each tear we shed, a sacrifice.
With faith as armor, our hearts are bold,
In sacred whispers, His truth foretold.

Transcending pain, we find our song,
With every struggle, we grow strong.
The path may twist, the journey long,
In unity, our spirits throng.

Through every storm, we find our peace,
In sacred moments, fears release.
Together we stand, in love we bind,
Transcending tribulation, hearts aligned.

In every heartbeat, He guides our way,
In difficult times, we choose to pray.
A tapestry of hope, we weave so pure,
Transcending all, His love ensures.

The Flame of Perseverance

In the depths of night, we rise,
Hope ignites beneath dark skies.
A flicker grows, a blaze of might,
Guiding us through endless fight.

Each step we take, a burning prayer,
With faith as fuel, we conquer despair.
Though winds may blow, and shadows stand,
We hold our ground, united we band.

Through trials fierce, our spirits soar,
With every flame, we seek for more.
In the heart of struggle, we find our call,
In the sacred light, we stand tall.

Voices whisper, "Do not yield,"
With every heartache, a shield revealed.
In unison, we break the chains,
Stronger together, through all the pains.

And when the dawn begins to break,
The fire within, no chance to shake.
For in the soul, a truth will gleam,
The flame of faith, our life's true dream.

With Every Breath of Faith

With every breath, a prayer we share,
In whispered hopes, we find our care.
Through trials faced, we seek the light,
In faith's embrace, our hearts take flight.

Each morning dawns, with grace anew,
In every moment, a chance to pursue.
The spirit sings, a sacred song,
With every breath, we belong.

Every heartbeat echoes love,
A testament to the skies above.
In trust we walk, on paths unseen,
With every breath, we breathe serene.

In silence deep, the soul will rise,
Finding solace in the skies.
Through valleys low and mountains high,
With every breath, we learn to fly.

So let us rise, where faith prevails,
Across the seas, through winds and gales.
With earnest hearts, we cast our fears,
With every breath, we'll dry our tears.

The Fortress of the Soul

Within our hearts, a fortress stands,
Built on trust and loving hands.
Through storms and trials, it does not fall,
In every shadow, we hear the call.

The walls are strong, with love entwined,
In grace and peace, our hearts aligned.
Through every rage, and endless night,
We find our strength, we find our light.

Each brick is laid with fervent prayer,
In unity, we rise and care.
As foes may come, they shall not breach,
In our fortress, hope shall teach.

When fear assails, and doubt draws near,
We hold our ground, in faith sincere.
For in the silence, we hear the sound,
Of whispers pure, our strength profound.

So let us stand, this fortress shield,
In times of trouble, it shall yield.
With hearts unbroken, spirits whole,
Together we thrive, the fortress of the soul.

Clad in the Spirit's Armor

Clad in the armor, our spirits rise,
With faith as shield 'neath endless skies.
In battles fought, both near and far,
We journey forth, our guiding star.

Each piece is forged with love and grace,
A perfect fit, our rightful place.
With courage bright, we face the storm,
In sacred trust, our hearts grow warm.

With steadfast hearts, we claim our ground,
In every challenge, hope is found.
In light and dark, the armor shines,
Protecting us, in life's designs.

Our spirits strong, we walk in peace,
With every moment, fears release.
Together bound, we fight as one,
Clad in the spirit, the battle won.

So let us stand, hearts intertwined,
In faith and love, the truth defined.
For in this armor, we shall not part,
With every beat, a faithful heart.

Anointed with Valor

In the glow of dawn's embrace,
Strength arises, filled with grace.
Hearts united, spirits soar,
Anointed warriors at heaven's door.

With each breath, faith ignites,
Guided by celestial lights.
Courage flows like rivers wide,
In valor bold, we abide.

Mountains tremble, shadows fade,
In our hearts, love is laid.
Through trials fierce, we stand tall,
For in our unity, we won't fall.

Voices lifted, praises sing,
Honor bestowed to our King.
With every battle, we prepare,
Armored in hope, free from despair.

Together, we rise, hand in hand,
In the garden of faith, we stand.
Anointed with valor, pure and bright,
We march onward, guided by light.

The Unfaltering Path

On the road where shadows creep,
Faithful footsteps, promises keep.
Through the darkness, we find our way,
Trusting in grace every day.

With every step, the heart beats strong,
In the silence, we hear the song.
A gentle whisper in the night,
Leading us onward toward the light.

The winds may howl, the storms may rage,
Still, we turn each solemn page.
Hoping for peace, we stand firm,
With love's flame, we'll always affirm.

In the trials that come our way,
We embrace each challenge and sway.
With eyes set on the distant shore,
We'll follow the path forevermore.

Together we walk, side by side,
In the spirit, our hearts abide.
On this journey, souls entwined,
The unfaltering path, divinely designed.

Heavenly Embrace

In tender moments, heaven's sigh,
Cherished souls begin to fly.
Wrapped in love, a sweet release,
Finding solace, heart's true peace.

Stars above, a guiding light,
In the quiet of the night.
Radiance shines from skies so deep,
Awakening dreams lost in sleep.

With open arms, grace descends,
Binding hearts, heaven sends.
A gentle touch, a whispered prayer,
In every breath, our spirits share.

The love of God, our refuge strong,
In this dance, we all belong.
Together, we rise, we embrace,
In every longing, seek His face.

Beneath the heavens, we're reborn,
In the light of faith, we are sworn.
Finding joy in each embrace,
With hearts united, we seek His face.

Beneath the Wings of Hope

Beneath the wings of hope we stand,
Faithful hearts, joined hand in hand.
In the tempest, we find our calm,
Wrapped in spirit, sweet as balm.

With every shadow, every fear,
Love surrounds us, drawing near.
In the darkest hour, we shine bright,
Trusting the dawn will bring the light.

Echoes of joy on the wind,
In harmony, our souls rescind.
Together we rise, lift the praise,
Navigating life's endless maze.

With every step, we journey on,
In the light, we are reborn.
Beneath those wings, we rest secure,
In hope's embrace, we are pure.

So let us sing, with hearts ablaze,
In faith, we'll walk through life's maze.
Together, forever, we will stand,
Beneath the wings of hope, so grand.

Cherished Strength

In quiet prayer, I find my peace,
A gentle whisper, my heart's release.
With every breath, I seek Your grace,
In trials faced, I see Your face.

Through storms that rage and shadows that fall,
Your love surrounds, I stand tall.
When burdens weigh on my weary soul,
Your strength within, it makes me whole.

With faith unyielding, I rise anew,
In darkest nights, Your light shines through.
Each struggle faced, I grow in might,
My cherished strength, my guiding light.

In silent moments, I hold on tight,
To promises made, and morning light.
With open heart, I journey far,
For You, O Lord, are my guiding star.

In strength I walk, though weak I be,
Your hand supports, it comforts me.
With every step, I trust and sing,
For in my heart, You are my King.

The Redeemed Resolve

With weary hearts, we seek Your grace,
In every trial, we find our place.
Through doubt and fear, we lift our eyes,
Your promise stands, our spirits rise.

In whispered prayers, we find our voice,
In every struggle, we make our choice.
To rise again, despite the fall,
In faith and love, we heed the call.

With hands held high, we face the fight,
For in our hearts, You are the light.
With every tear, our spirits mend,
In You, O Lord, we find our friend.

Through valleys deep, our steps are sure,
In hope and trust, our hearts endure.
Redeemed by grace, we stand as one,
Our resolve is set, Your will be done.

In unity, our voices raise,
A chorus sung to sing Your praise.
In every heart, Your love will dwell,
The redeemed resolve, we know too well.

Inspired by Faith

In every moment, I choose to see,
The beauty of life, the gift of Thee.
With faith as my anchor, I stand so tall,
In love's embrace, I will not fall.

In gentle whispers, Your truth unfolds,
A story of grace that never grows old.
With every heartbeat, I'm reminded anew,
That all my strength, O Lord, is You.

In fields of doubt, I sow the seed,
With kindness and hope, I plant the need.
Inspired by faith, I walk the way,
In Your embrace, I find my stay.

Through trials faced, my spirit grows,
In every challenge, Your love shows.
With arms wide open, I greet the day,
Inspired by faith, I kneel and pray.

With courage burning, I rise and soar,
For in Your presence, I seek for more.
Inspired by faith, I live and breathe,
In trust and hope, my heart believes.

The Radiance of Resilience

In shadows cast, a light will gleam,
Through trials fought, we dare to dream.
The radiance of resilience shines,
A testament of love, divine signs.

With every setback, we rise once more,
In faith, we find an open door.
Through storms that shake, our spirits soar,
The radiance of hope forever more.

In moments bleak, we stand as one,
In every battle, the victory's begun.
With hearts ablaze, our souls ignite,
In the radiance of love, we take flight.

Together we rise, no fear shall bind,
In every challenge, new strength we find.
The radiance of resilience glows,
With courage steadfast, our journey flows.

In the light of dawn, we claim our place,
In every heartbeat, we see Your grace.
The radiance of resilience, our guiding chart,
In every struggle, we find our heart.

Spirit Unbroken

In trials faced, we rise anew,
With faith as guide, our hearts hold true.
Beneath the storm, we find our way,
In sacred light, we trust and pray.

Though burdens heavy weigh on soul,
In every crack, He makes us whole.
With gentle hands, He molds our strife,
A symphony of strength and life.

Through darkest valleys, paths unclear,
His voice will whisper, 'Do not fear.'
Rays of hope break through the night,
Our spirit shines, embracing light.

On wings of grace, we soar above,
In hearts united, we share His love.
No pain can break our holy bond,
In every heartbeat, we respond.

Together we stand, steadfast and bold,
With stories of faith, in hearts retold.
In unity, our voices rise,
A testament to the skies.

The Power of the Faithful

In whispered prayers, our hearts align,
With fervent hope, a sacred sign.
Through trials faced, we stand as one,
In love's embrace, our battles won.

The faithful gather, hand in hand,
In joyous grace, we take our stand.
With courage deep, we forge our path,
In every heart, ignites His wrath.

Together we sing, a hymn of praise,
In tranquil nights and sunlit days.
With open arms, we share His light,
A beacon bright, within the night.

Through shadows cast, we find His way,
With truth and love, we shall not sway.
In every soul, His presence dwells,
In hearts profound, His story tells.

So let us rise, with spirits strong,
In faith we trust, where we belong.
With every step, we journey forth,
In harmony, we share His worth.

Whispers of Divine Might

The winds that blow, they carry peace,
With whispers soft, our fears release.
In every moment, grace bestowed,
In silent prayers, our hearts explode.

The mountains tall, a testament,
To strength divine, in each ascent.
Through trials fierce, He stands with us,
In faith's embrace, we choose to trust.

From creeks that flow, to skies that shine,
In every tear, He draws the line.
With every heartbeat, love renews,
In tenderness, His light imbues.

In gentle sighs, we find our rest,
In His embrace, we are most blessed.
With grace abounding, we shall rise,
Triumphant songs, we lift to skies.

So hear the call, His voice is clear,
In faith's great love, we banish fear.
With hearts aflame, we journey on,
In sacred trust, our fears are gone.

In the Shadow of the Almighty

In twilight's grace, we seek His face,
In shadows deep, we find our place.
Amidst the trials that life bestows,
His sheltering arms, our refuge flows.

With every heartbeat, whispers near,
In sacred silence, He calms our fear.
The strength we claim, in Him we find,
With every thought, He fills our mind.

Through raging storms, we hold our ground,
In faith's embrace, our hope is found.
With every prayer, our spirits rise,
In unity, we seek the skies.

In darkest hours, His light breaks through,
With every dawn, our hearts renew.
The promises made, forever true,
In love unbound, we are made new.

So under shadows, we shall tread,
With spirits soaring where angels led.
In every trial, His might will show,
In shadows deep, our love will grow.

The Path Less Wandered

In shadows deep, where few have trod,
Faith lights the way, it is our mod.
Through trials faced and mountains steep,
We find our strength, in silence keep.

With every step, our spirits rise,
In humble hearts, the truth complies.
Though thorns may pierce, and storms do rage,
Divine embrace, we turn the page.

The path unfolds as night gives way,
Hope is the dawn, a bright array.
In whispered prayers, we seek the grace,
The journey guides, we find our place.

Through doubts and fears, we walk with love,
Embracing light that's sent from above.
For every tear that marks our face,
A seed of faith, we find our space.

The path less wandered, blessed and true,
In unity found, our spirits grew.
With hearts ablaze, we take the lead,
On sacred ground, we plant the seed.

The Gift of Grit

In trials faced, we pray for might,
Our spirits strong, we seek the light.
Through darkest nights, our hope we cling,
With every breath, our voices sing.

With grit bestowed, we rise anew,
In faith's embrace, our strength we grew.
When fears surround, we stand our ground,
In every heart, resilience found.

Each battle fought is not in vain,
For through the storm, we break the chain.
With steadfast hearts, we chase our dreams,
The gift of grit, our spirit beams.

In unity's bond, we stand as one,
Through shadows cast, the journey's spun.
Together we rise, in love abide,
The gift of grit, our faithful guide.

A Testament of Triumph

With hands uplifted, we seek to rise,
In every trial, a sweet disguise.
For in the struggle, we find our way,
A testament of triumph, come what may.

Through ashes deep, our hopes reborn,
In every loss, our hearts are worn.
Yet courage blooms in team and grace,
A brighter dawn, a sacred place.

With each small victory, faith we gain,
A light that shines amidst the pain.
In every heartbeat, a song we sing,
A testament of triumph, our offering.

From doubts released, we claim our fate,
In every moment, we participate.
United strong, through thick and thin,
A testament of triumph, love shall win.

Wings of Tenacity

In trials faced, we learn to soar,
With wings of tenacity, we explore.
Through storms that rage and tempests wild,
Our hearts are bold, like a fearless child.

With faith embedded in every flight,
We chase the dreams that burn so bright.
Through winds of change, we glide with grace,
Wings of tenacity, a sacred space.

In unity found, we take the leap,
Through valleys low, and mountains steep.
For though we stumble, we rise again,
On wings of tenacity, free from pain.

With every challenge, we find our song,
A choir raised, we all belong.
So let us fly, with hearts so free,
On wings of tenacity, we shall be.

Our journey leads to heights unknown,
In love's embrace, our spirits grown.
Together we rise, through joy and strife,
Wings of tenacity, the dance of life.

Milton Keynes UK
Ingram Content Group UK Ltd.
UKHW020041271124
451585UK00012B/975